Little Critters
Praying Mantises

by Lisa J. Amstutz

CAPSTONE PRESS
a capstone imprint

Little Pebble is published by Capstone Press,
1710 Roe Crest Drive, North Mankato, Minnesota 56003
www.mycapstone.com

Library of Congress Cataloging-in-Publication Data

Names: Amstutz, Lisa J., author.
Title: Praying mantises / by Lisa Amstutz.
Other titles: Little pebble. Little critters.
Description: North Mankato, Minnesota : Capstone Press, a Capstone imprint,
  [2018] | Series: Little pebble. Little critters | Audience: Ages 4–8. |
  Audience: K to grade 3. | Includes bibliographical references and index.
Identifiers: LCCN 2016051634| ISBN 9781515778257 (library binding) | ISBN
  9781515778387 (pbk.) | ISBN 9781515778424 (eBook PDF)
Subjects: LCSH: Praying mantis—Juvenile literature.
Classification: LCC QL505.9.M35 A47 2018 | DDC 595.7/27—dc23
LC record available at https://lccn.loc.gov/2016051634

Editorial Credits

Gena Chester, editor; Sarah Bennett, designer; Wanda Winch, media researcher;
Tori Abraham, production specialist

Photo Credits

Dreamstime: Wxgtupian, 11; Shutterstock: Auschara Roongthanasub, plant leaves background,
Eric Isselee, 3, 24, Evgeniy Ayupov, 19, Florian Andronache, 21, iava777, cover, Kristina
Postnikova, 13, Lightspring, 5, Muhammad Naaim, 1, Paul Looyen, 9, Rob Byron, 7, Ryan M.
Bolton, 17, Valeria73, 15, Yousef Abuaisheh, 22

Table of Contents

Hiding 4

Good Hunters 12

Growing Up 16

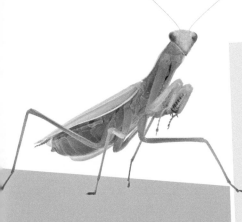

Glossary 22
Read More 23
Internet Sites 23
Critical Thinking Questions . . 24
Index 24

Hiding

Is that a leaf?

No! It is a praying mantis!

The mantis matches a plant.
Hungry animals will not see it.

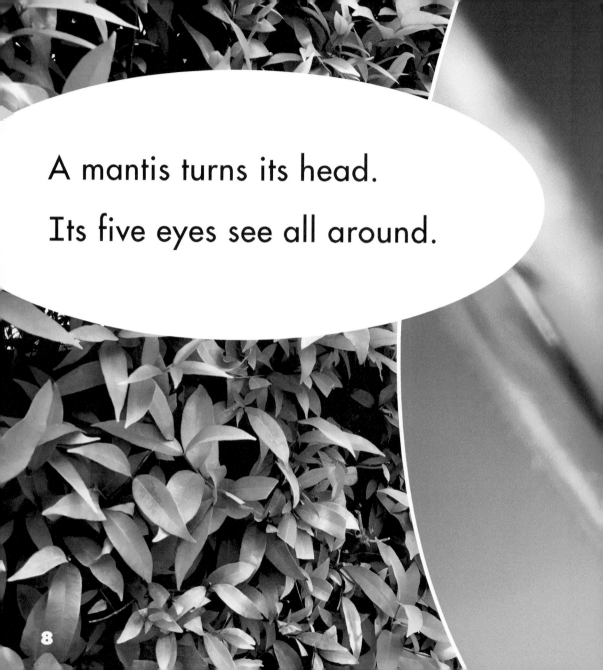

A mantis turns its head.

Its five eyes see all around.

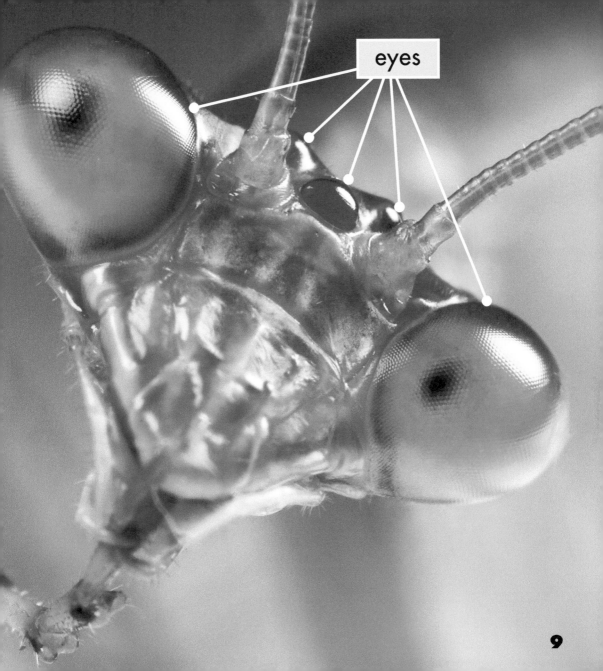

eyes

Look out!

A hungry bat is near.

Hiss! The mantis scares

the bat away.

Good Hunters

Snatch!

Spiny front legs grab prey.

They hold on tight. Chomp!

Yum!

Mantises eat bugs.

They eat small birds too.

They even eat each other!

Growing Up

A female lays eggs on a twig. The eggs are in a case. It keeps them safe.

Babies hatch out.

They look like small adults.

But they have no wings.

The babies grow fast.

Soon they fly. Bye!

Glossary

adult—an animal that is fully grown

case—an outer covering

hatch—to break out of an egg

insect—a small animal with a hard outer shell, six legs, three body sections, and two antennae; most insects have wings

prey—an animal hunted by another animal for food

spiny—covered with sharp spines

Read More

Borgert-Spaniol, Megan. *Praying Mantises.* Creepy Crawlies. Minneapolis, Bellwether Media, 2016.

Hesper, Sam. *Praying Mantises.* Animal Cannibals. New York: PowerKids Press, 2015.

Maley, Adrienne Houk. *20 Fun Facts About Praying Mantises.* New York: Gareth Stevens, Inc., 2013.

Internet Sites

FactHound offers a safe, fun way to find Internet sites related to this book. All of the sites on FactHound have been researched by our staff.

Here's all you do:
Visit *www.facthound.com*
Type in this code: 9781515778257

Check out projects, games and lots more at
www.capstonekids.com

Critical Thinking Questions

1. What do praying mantises eat?

2. How do praying mantises avoid being eaten?

3. How is a baby praying mantis the same as an adult? How is it different?

Index

babies, 18, 20

bats, 10

eating, 14

eggs, 16

eyes, 8

head, 8

legs, 12

matching, 6

prey, 12

safety, 16

wings, 18